To: Jaden

From: Jaden

Table Of Contents

17

I return. Two years of empty pages
Different setting, many changes
Many seasons, many rages
I feel the same among the ages

Many visions, many rights
Many wrongs, many nights
The rain is pouring out my tears
The trees grow, the sun appears

Little time, I see the light
I want to win, I want to fight *

Risks

I stand. 100 feet up on the edge
Fresh water 100 feet below
My throat is dry, my skin is cracked
Dehydration eager to grow

Years and years of waiting
For this moment, chance slim
But I search for a way out, a safe way down
I can't swim

I stand on the edge of the edge
The edge of time, time is ticking
I throw my hands up to pray to God
If God is listening

I'm on the cliff of comfortability
A sickly place on a pretty stump
Quickly I make up my mind
One step forward and
I jump. *

Love?

What is love?
If it hurts, what do we gain?
Is one year of endearment
Worth a lifetime of pain?

Many would say love is an action
A verb
But if every "I love you"
Came with different actions
Would love then just be a word? *

<u>Who</u>

Who's that person in my mind?
Who's that person deep inside?
Pushing me into the sea
Of thoughts, the words surrounding me
Who's that person in my head?
Claiming the past has value instead
Of the present and all that lies ahead
It's me- the enemy and victim interbred *

The Mirror

The clearest of glass
To show your reflection
Yet each day it tricks you
With an easy objection
But it's really because of
Your own self deception that
Each day it tells you
You're a different person
Because of your own
Inconsistent self perception *

The War Within

Life is an everlasting war
The worst battle being within
Self vs. self, me vs. me
A really hard battle to win *

(The War Within) Mini Monologue:

If someone is always angry
They shouldn't be told to "stop being so angry"
If someone is always serious
They shouldn't be told to "stop being so serious"
If someone is always unhappy
They shouldn't be told to "just be happy"
Most likely if they're always that way, it's because
They don't know how to express themselves in other ways
They need to be GUIDED and not made
To feel as if no one understands and be forced
Back into the hole that they dug around themselves
Just because one person doesn't deal with
Another person's battles,
it doesn't make theirs any less challenging or less significant...

I Like My Hair

I like my hair
The different styles
Curly, straight,
Dark, and wild

I like my eyes
Big and round
I see the world
A sight profound

I like my mouth
The right to speak
To have a voice that's
Distinct, unique *

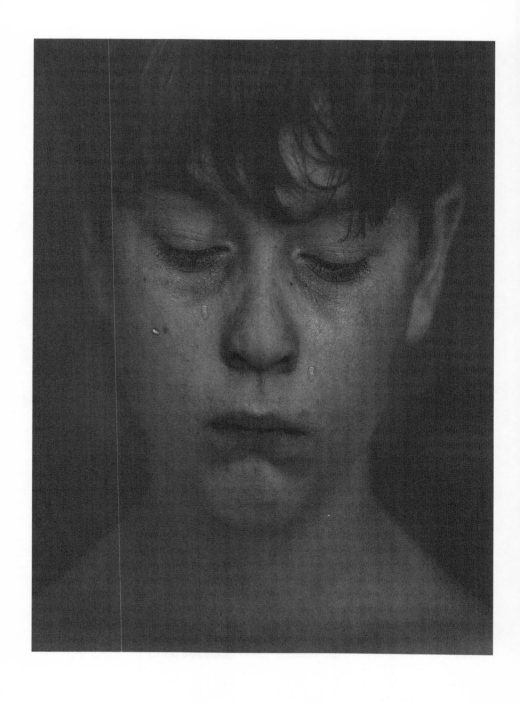

<u>Sometimes</u>

Sometimes we sing
Sometimes we dance
Sometimes we leave
Things up to chance
Sometimes we just buy and buy
And sometimes...
We cry and we don't know why *

Friends

Best friends are the ones
That have left me behind
Close friends are the ones
That are hard to find
Friendships are short
Only the best ones last
Only the real ones can stay
Only true friends can pass
The test of time
Old seasons turned new
And I may not have many
But thank God I have a few *

<u>I'm Afraid</u>

I'm afraid of the unknown
Guess we can all say so
But I'm also afraid of the truth
And I'm just as afraid to know
What I'll find deep inside
Beneath the layers of my skin
The things that have been hidden
Overtime from way back when *

The Rotten Tree Pt.1

There is a rotten tree
That rises to the sky
Twisted in every way
It's roots thick and wide

It stirs up a storm
Brings on the rain
Turns the clouds gray
Takes all that's sane

By this tree, I must stay
With water, I must give
No where else I will lay
With its fruit, I will live *

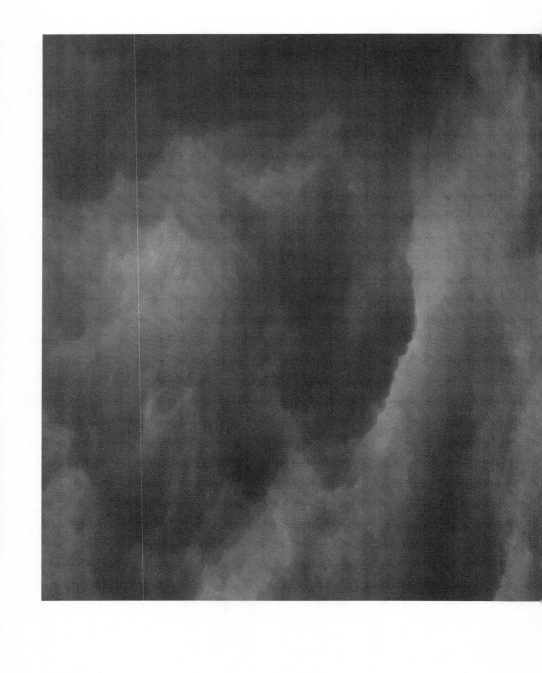

The Rotten Tree Pt.2

But then the sky changed
The clouds got darker
The green leaves fell
The wind blew harder
The rotten tree withered away
The trunk torn at the root
I jumped up to grab the branches
I hated the tree but needed its fruit
Too late, lightning struck
Zapping everything into ashes
So I stand alone in the dark
In my room, my mind crashes *

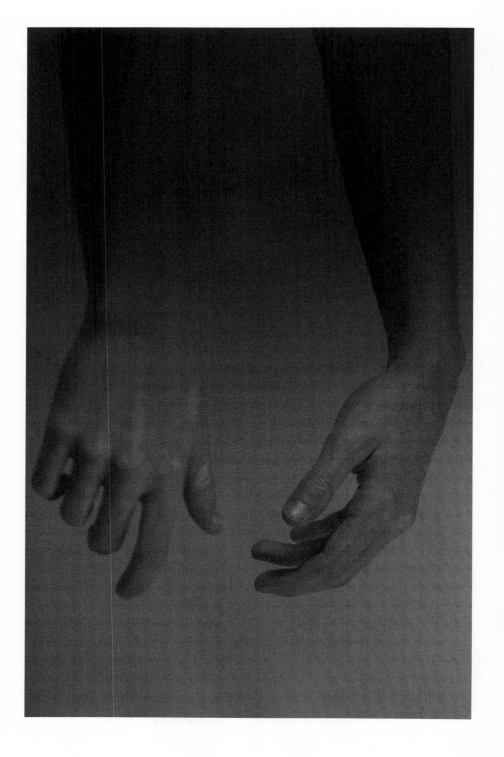

His Finger Was Blue

I remember that day
That exact very moment
His hands were hard as stone
Frozen
Frozen and empty
Frozen and empty
Frozen and empty
It's own deadly symphony
Then I noticed
Something bizarre and wrong
His finger was blue
And that's how I knew
That he was gone *

<u>Light</u>

They say there's always light
At the end of the tunnel
But not at night
When the sun goes down

They say there's always light
At the end of the tunnel
But no light in sight
Can make anyone drown

Yet the light always penetrates
The darkest darkness
And the sun always rises once again *

<u>Uncertain Certainty</u>

I'm uncertainly certain
I'm certain of the uncertainty
It's great to have plans
But plans change inevitably

I thought I knew before
And I thought I saw ahead
And I thought I dreamed
Of the dreams by which
My future was led
But I was wrong.
Now I have uncertain certainty *

Meditate

I close my eyes
Take one breath in
Take one breath out
And count to ten
I hope and pray
For a peace to find
I focus and
Leave the thoughts behind
An attempt to control
My preoccupied mind *

In Conclusion

In conclusion, life goes on
With lessons learned
And hearts torn
There can never ever be enough planning
So in conclusion, there is no conclusion
Our souls are infinite
Forever standing *

Made in the USA
Columbia, SC
01 June 2020